GRADE 1

Fluency FIRST!™

Timothy Rasinski • Nancy Padak

The McGraw-Hill Companies

www.WrightGroup.com

Fluency First! Daily Routines to Develop Reading Fluency: Grade 1

Created by Kent Publishing Services, Inc.
Designed by Signature Design Group, Inc.
Illustrations by Marilyn Barr, Shirely Beckes, Nelle Davis, and Steve Sullivan

The publishers would like to acknowledge the authors and publishers of the following copyrighted works, which appear in *Fluency First!* Grade 1 Student Book. Page 14, "September" by Lucille Clifton. Copyright © by Lucille Clifton. First appeared in *Everett Anderson's Year*, published by Henry Holt and Company. Reprinted by permission of Curtis Brown, Ltd.; page 62, "Little Piece of Prickly Pear" by Tony Johnston, "Little Piece of Prickly Pear/Pedacito de nopal, text" from MY MEXICO/MEXICO MIO by Tony Johnston, copyright © 1996 by Roger D. Johnson and Susan T. Johnson as Trustees of the Johnson Family Trust, text. Used by permission of G.P. Putnam's Sons, A Division of Penguin Young Readers Group, A Member of Penguin Group (USA) Inc., 345 Hudson Street, New York, NY 10014. All rights reserved.; page 64, "The Pickety Fence" by David McCord, From ONE AT A TIME by David McCord. Copyright © 1965, 1966 by David McCord. By permission of Little, Brown and Co., Inc.; page 66, "Rain" by Sonja Dunn, Pembroke Publishers; page 74, "City Bus" by Sonja Dunn, Pembroke Publishers; page 78, "Covers" by Nikki Giovanni; page 90, "Tommy" by Gwendolyn Brooks. *Reprinted By Consent of Brooks Permissions.*; page 92, "My People" by Langston Hughes, "My People", from THE COLLECTED POEMS OF LANGSTON HUGHES by Langston Hughes, copyright © 1994 by The Estate of Langston Hughes. Used by permission of Alfred A. Knopf, a division of Random House, Inc.; page 98, "Every Six Months" by Sonja Dunn, Pembroke Publishers; page 108, "Kookaburra Sits in the Old Gum Tree" by Marion Sinclair. KOOKABURRA SITS IN THE OLD GUM TREE, Words and Music by Marion Sinclair. Copyright © 1934 (Renewed) Larrikin Music Pub. Pty. Ltd. All Rights Administered by Music Sales Corporation for the Western Hemisphere. International Copyright Secured. All Rights Reserved. Reprinted by Permission.; page 114, "Sorry, Sorry Mrs. Lorry" by Nannette Mellage; page 122, "Beetle Thoughts" by Aileen Fisher, "Beetle Thoughts" from Out in the Dark and Daylight by Aileen Fisher. Copyright © 1980 Aileen Fisher. Used by permission of Marian Reiner on behalf of the Boulder Public Library Foundation, Inc.; page 126, "All Aboard" by Fay Robinson, McGraw-Hill; page 138, "Andre" by Gwendolyn Brooks. *Reprinted By Consent of Brooks Permissions.*; page 144, "Fruit Salad" by Anastasia Suen, McGraw-Hill; page 150, "Goodbye" by Sonja Dunn, Pembroke Publishers.

Printed in the United States of America.

Send all inquiries to:
Wright Group/McGraw-Hill
P.O. Box 812960
Chicago, IL 60681

ISBN: 1-4045-2664-1

5 6 7 8 9 10 MAZ 10 09 08 07

Table of Contents

Table of Contents *continued*

Introduction

This is How Fluency First! Lessons Work

 Listen

 Read Along

 Practice in Class

Practice at Home

Build Your Skills

Perform

Skip to My Lou

Skip, skip,
Skip to my Lou!
Skip, skip,
Skip to my Lou!
Skip to my Lou, my darling!

Flies in the buttermilk,
Shoo! shoo! shoo!
Flies in the buttermilk,
Shoo! shoo! shoo!
Flies in the buttermilk,
Shoo! shoo! shoo!
Skip to my Lou, my darling!

American folk song

How did I read?

Rhyming Words

1. Write two new words that rhyme with these words from the poem.

to ______ ______

skip ______ ______

Complete the Words

2. Write the beginning letter to make four words from the poem.

___ou ___kip

___lies ___arling

Three Little Kittens

Three little kittens lost their mittens,
    and they began to cry,
"Oh, mother, dear, we sadly fear,
    Our mittens we have lost!"

"What! lost your mittens,
    you naughty kittens!
Then you shall have no pie."
    "Meow, meow, meow!"

Mother Goose

Sort the Words

1. Sort the words by the number of syllables, or beats, you hear. Write the words in the correct column.

little	pie	mittens	cry
lost	kittens	fear	meow

one syllable	two syllables

Two Little Apples

Two little apples hanging on a tree,
Two little apples smiling at me.

I shook that tree as hard as I could.
Down came the apples, Mm! Mm! Good!

Anonymous

Opposite and Same

1. Write a word from the poem to complete each sentence.

The opposite of **up** is ______________.

Small means the same as ______________.

The opposite of **bad** is ______________.

Rhyming Words

2. Write words from the poem that rhyme with each word.

bee ______________ ______________

wood ______________ ______________

September

I already know where Africa is
and I already know how to
count to ten and
I went to school every day last year,
why do I have to go again?

Lucille Clifton

Riddle Fun

1. Write words from the box into the word shapes to answer the questions.

school	ten	why	again

Which is a number word?

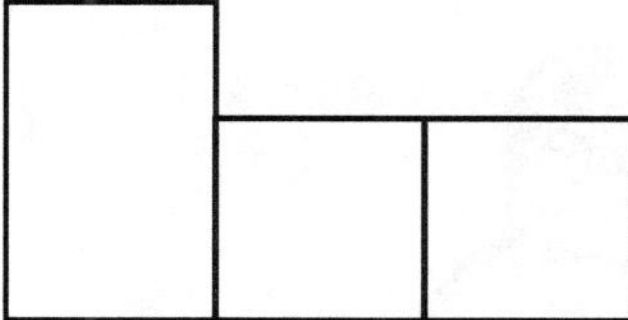

Which is a question word?

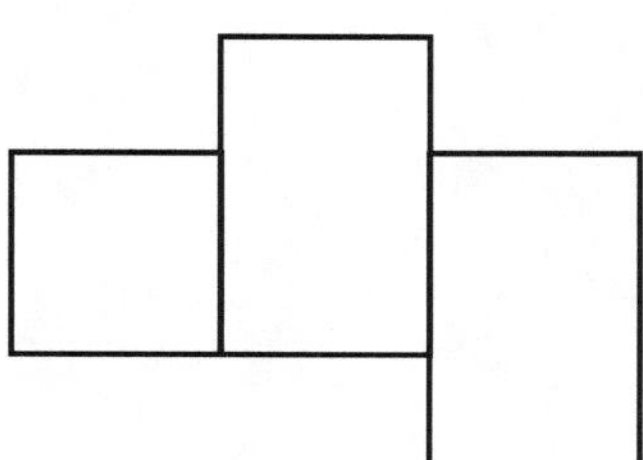

Which word means **another time**?

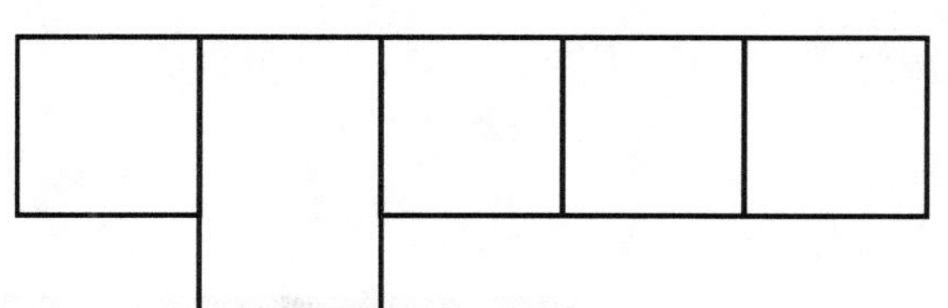

Which word names a place where you learn?

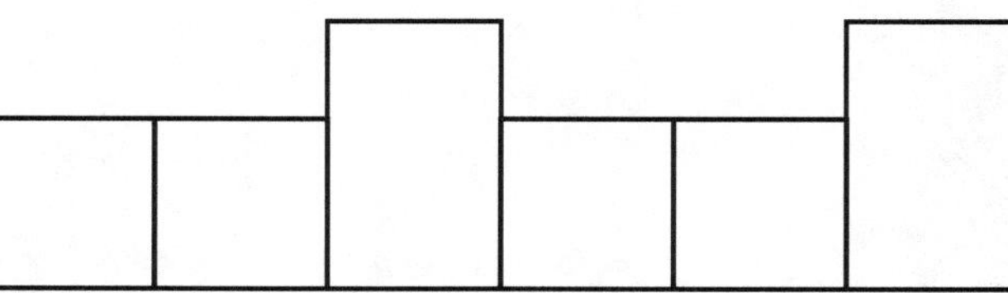

Bug in a Jug

Curious fly,
Vinegar jug,
Slippery edge,
Pickled bug.

Anonymous

New Beginning

1. Change the beginning letter in each word to make a word from the poem.

furious ______ rug ______

tickled ______

2. Change one letter in **fly** to make a word that means **a way to cook potatoes**. ______

Word Search

3. Write a word from the poem that means **a kind of insect**. ______

4. Write a word from the poem that is another name for **insect**. ______

Once I Saw a Little Bird

Once I saw a little bird
    Come hop, hop, hop;
So I cried, "Little bird,
    Will you stop, stop, stop?"

And I was going to the window
    To say, "How do you do?"
But he shook his little tail,
    And far away he flew.

Mother Goose

Rhyming Words

1. Write a word from the poem that rhymes with each word.

stop ______ look ______

mail ______ blew ______

New Beginning

2. Take **st** off the word **stop**. Add **dr**. Write and say the new word. ______

Count the Syllables

3. Circle the words that have two syllables or beats.

little shook window flew

Billy Button

Billy Button bought a buttered biscuit.
Did Billy Button buy a buttered biscuit?
If Billy Button bought a buttered biscuit,
Where's the buttered biscuit Billy Button bought?

Anonymous

Change the Word

1. Change a vowel in each word to write a word from the poem.

belly ____________ bay ____________

Ending Sounds

2. Say the words. Circle two that end with the same sound.

button biscuit bought

Sound-Alikes

3. Write a word from the poem that sounds the same but is spelled differently.

by ____________

Popcorn

Pop, pop, pop, pop,
Will it ever stop, stop, stop, stop?
Little puffs of popcorn
With butter on the top, top, top, top.

When it is all done, done, done, done,
Will you give me some, some, some, some?
Then I'll eat my popcorn
One by one by one by one.

Karen McGuigan Brothers

Change the Word

1. Change the first letter in **pop** to make words that complete the sentences.

My pet bunny likes to __________.

I cleaned up the spill with a __________.

I like to spin my __________.

Rhyming Words

2. Write words from the poem that rhyme with **fun**.

3. Write a word from the poem that rhymes with **fly**.

Old Mother Hubbard

Old Mother Hubbard
Went to the cupboard
To fetch her poor dog a bone;

But when she came there
The cupboard was bare,
And so the poor dog had none.

Mother Goose

Rhyming Words

1. Write a word from the poem that rhymes with each word.

sent ______ log ______

fame ______ care ______

2. Write two words from the box that rhyme with **bone**.

cone	one	done	tone

______ ______

Count the Syllables

3. Circle the words that have two syllables or beats.

fetch cupboard poor Hubbard

The Star

Twinkle, twinkle, little star,
How I wonder what you are!
Up above the world so high,
Like a diamond in the sky.

When the blazing sun is gone,
When he nothing shines upon,
Then you show your little light,
Twinkle, twinkle, all the night.

Jane and Ann Taylor

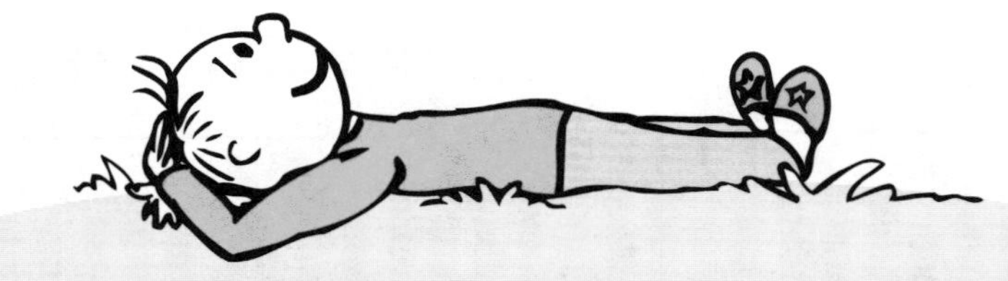

Change the Word

1. Change the first letter in each of these words to write a word from the poem.

ponder ______ hike ______

fun ______ right ______

Finish the Sentence

2. Write the word from the poem that completes each sentence.

Stars twinkle during the ______.

A star looks like a ______ in the sky.

Hey, Diddle, Diddle

Hey, diddle, diddle,
The cat and the fiddle,
The cow jumped over the moon;
The little dog laughed
To see such sport,
And the dish ran away with the spoon.

Mother Goose

Rhyming Words

1. Write two pairs of words from the poem that rhyme.

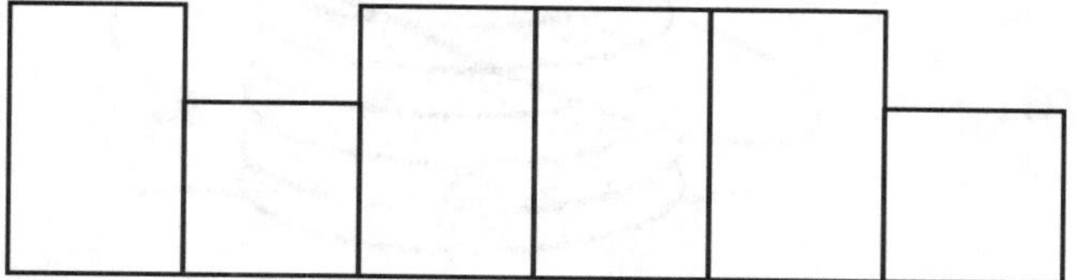
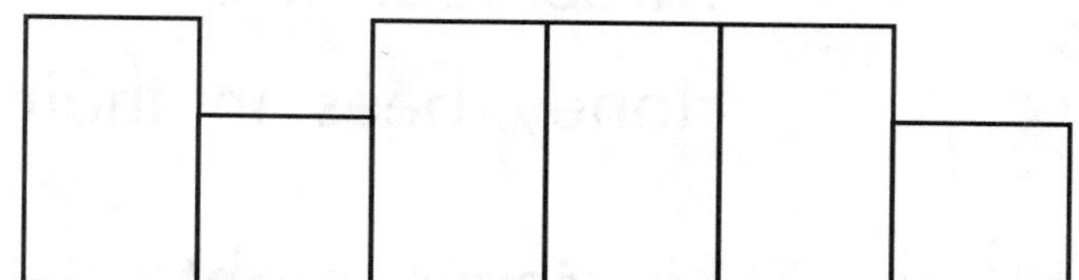

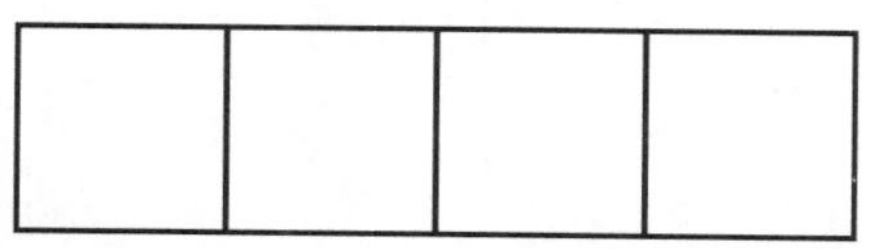
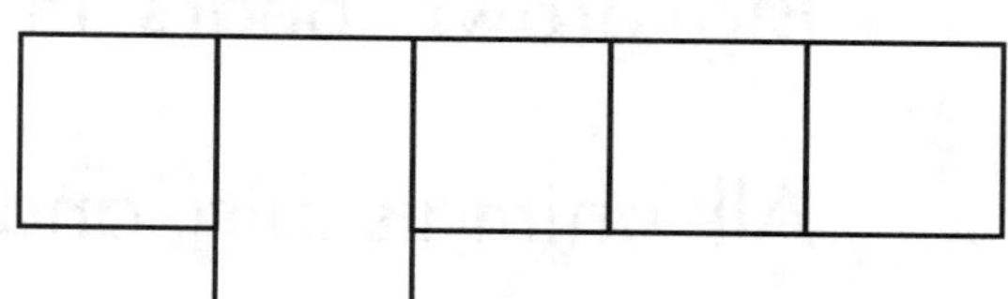

Match the Picture

2. Write the word from the box that matches each picture.

cow	dish	spoon

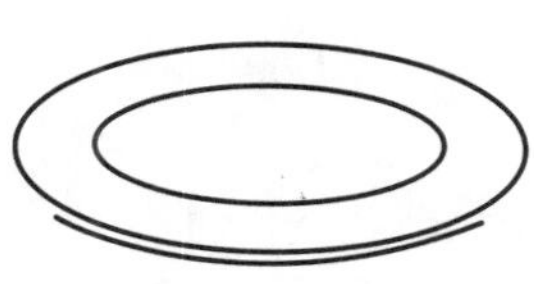

Homes

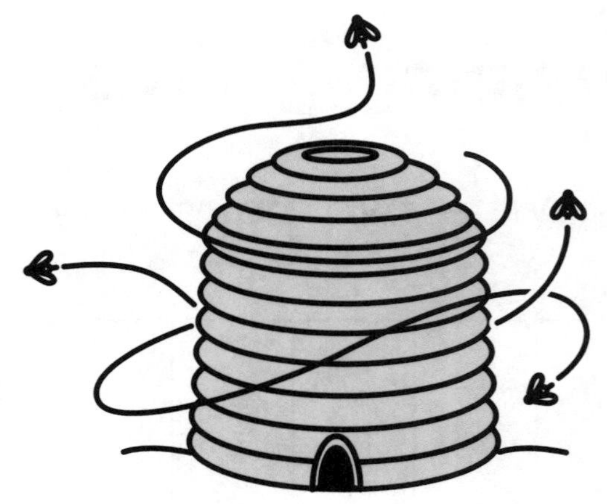

One two three
Three four five
Honey bees in their hive.

Six seven eight
Eight nine ten
Big brown bears in their den.

All animals big and small
Need a place that they can call
Home for one and home for all
Hive and den and pen and stall.

Tim Rasinski

Match the Picture

1. Write the word from the box that matches each picture.

den
hive
pen
stall

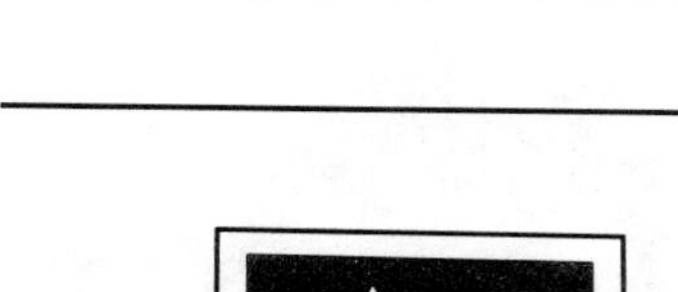

Complete the Sentence

2. Write the word that completes each sentence.

The bear's ______________ is in a cave.

The horse's ______________ is in the barn.

I Eat My Peas with Honey

I eat my peas with honey;
I've done it all my life.
It makes the peas taste funny,
But it keeps them on the knife.

Anynomous

Shape Search

1. Write two words from the poem that name things we eat.

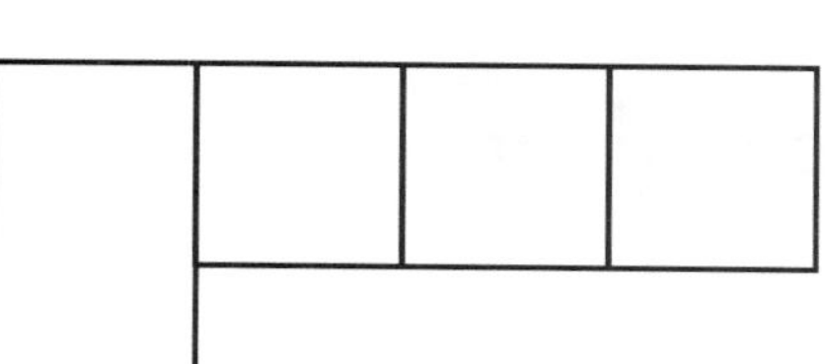

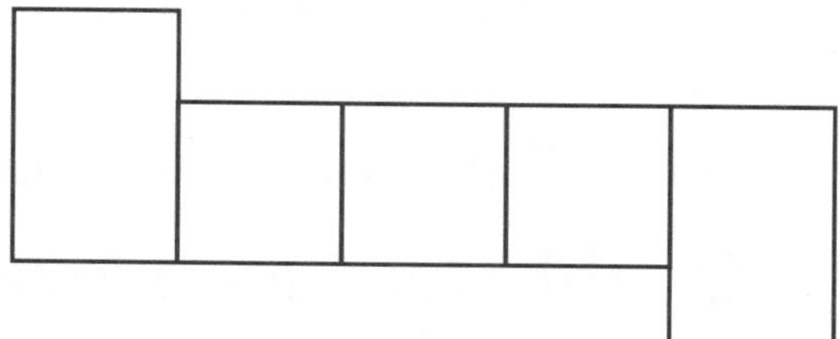

Drawing Pictures

2. Draw a picture for each word.

eat

honey

Five Little Seashells

Five little seashells lying on the shore;
Swish! went the waves,
    and then there were four.

Four little seashells, cozy as could be;
Swish! went the waves,
    and then there were three.

Three little seashells, all pearly new;
Swish! went the waves,
    and then there were two.

Two little seashells sleeping in the sun;
Swish! went the waves,
    and then there was one.

One little seashell left all alone;
It whispered "Shhhh"
    as I took it home.

Counting rhyme

Match it Up

1. Draw a line to match each word with a picture.

four

seashell

waves

home

Counting Words

2. How many words are in each sentence?
Write the number on the line.

Swish! went the waves,
and then there were four. ______

It whispered "Shhhh"
as I took it home. ______

Take Me Out to the Ball Game

Take me out to the ball game,
Take me out to the crowd,
Buy me some peanuts and cracker jack,
I don't care if I ever get back.

Let me root, root, root for the home team,
If they don't win, it's a shame,
For it's one, two, three strikes, you're out
At the old ball game.

Jack Norworth

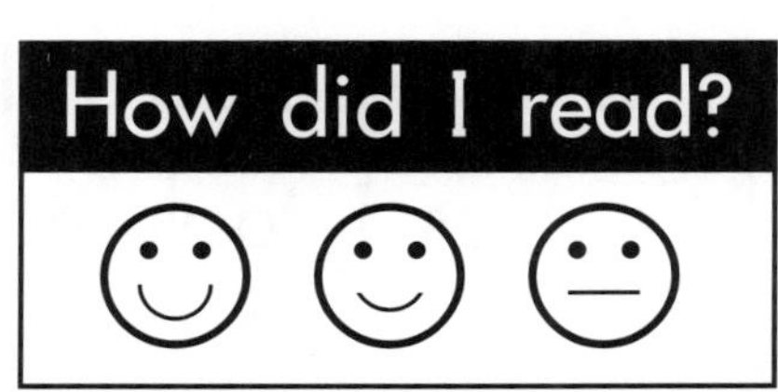

Shape Search

1. Write the letters that complete each word from the poem.

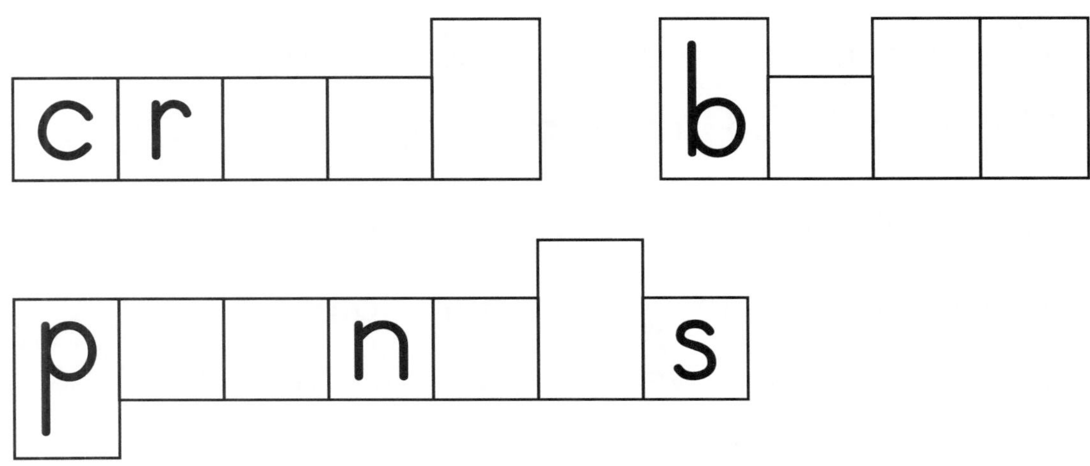

Complete the Sentence

2. Write the word that completes each sentence.

I don't care if I ever get ________________.

If they don't win, it's a ________________.

One, two, three ________________, you're out!

This Is the Way We Wash Our Hands

This is the way we wash our hands,
Wash our hands, wash our hands,
This is the way we wash our hands,
On a cold and frosty morning.

This is the way we wash our clothes,
Wash our clothes, wash our clothes,
This is the way we wash our clothes,
On a cold and frosty morning.

Mother Goose

Shape Search

1. Write three words from the poem that start with **w**.

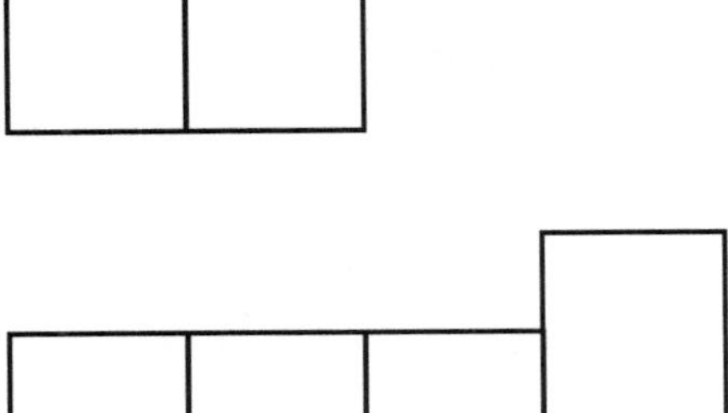

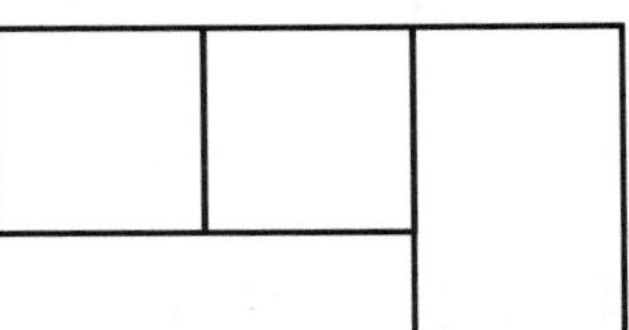

Description Words

2. Write two words from the poem that describe the morning.

What to Wash

3. Write two words from the poem that tell what we wash.

Cat on a Log

Jump! jump! went the frog.
"Ruff, ruff," said the dog.
"Oinky, oink, oink," squealed the hog.
Cat just sat like a bump on a log.

Tim Rasinski

Riddle Fun

1. Answer each question with the name of an animal. Write it on the line.

I sit like a bump on a log.
Who am I?

I say, "ruff, ruff."
Who am I?

I say, "oinky, oink, oink."
Who am I?

I go jump, jump.
Who am I?

Describe Cats

2. Write three describing words about cats below.

Words

One, two, three, four, five...
A, B, C, D, E...
Blue, red, green, yellow, orange...
Cow, cat, dog, fish, bee...
Words are things I learn in school.
Words are things I know.
I learn new words with every day,
Words that help me grow.

Sarah Hutt

Shape Search

1. Write three words from the poem that are names of colors.

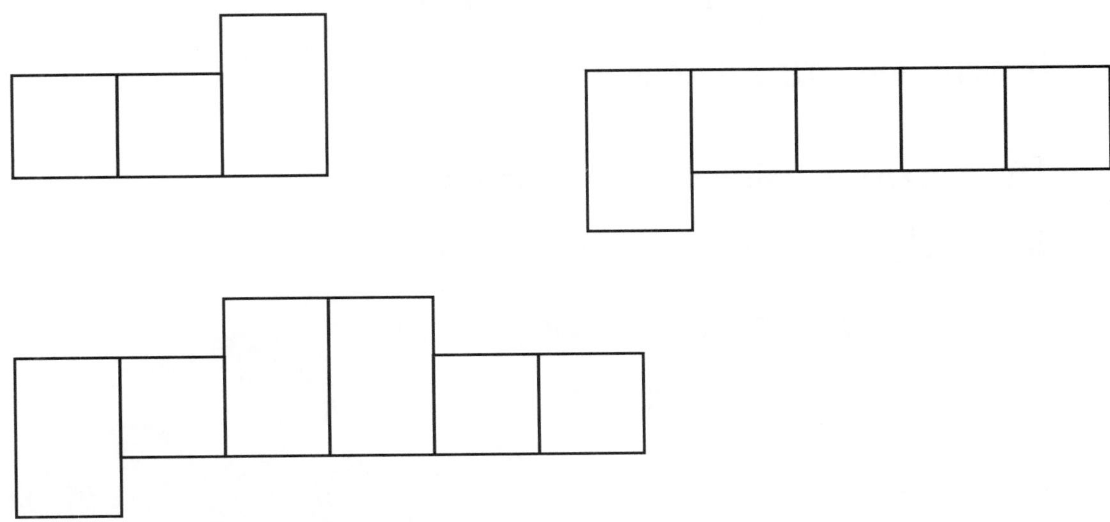

Which Is Which?

2. Draw a line from the word to the picture that it matches.

cow

cat

dog

fish

We're Going to the Orchard

We are going to the orchard,
To see how apples grow.
We are going to the orchard,
It will be fun, I know.

The farmer picks the apples,
Just when their time is right.
I hope he cuts some apples up,
So we can have a bite.

Karen McGuigan Brothers

How did I read?

Match the Action

1. Label each picture with an action word from the box.

cut	bite	pick

Write the Word

2. What is growing in the orchard? Write the word below.

Baby Bumblebee

Oh, I'm bringing home a baby bumblebee
Won't my mommy be so proud of me
'Cause I'm bringing home a baby
bumblebee—
Buzzy, buzzy, buzzy—
OOOOH, it bit me!

Oh, I'm bringing home a baby rattlesnake
Won't my mommy shiver and shake
'Cause I'm bringing home a
baby rattlesnake—
Rattle, rattle, rattle—
OOOOH, it bit me!

Author unknown

Same Sound

1. Say the word. Write another word from the poem that starts with the same sound.

baby

my

shiver

Write the Word

2. Complete the words to name the animals mommy will soon see.

a baby bumble

a baby rattle

Ten Tom-Toms

Ten tom-toms,
Timpani, too,
Ten tall tubas
And an old kazoo

Ten trombones—
Give them a hand!
The sitting-standing-marching-running
Big Brass Band

Author unknown

Word Sort

1. Write and say words from the poem.

Words that begin with **t**

Words that begin with **s**

Words that begin with **b**

A Lively Young Fisher

A lively young fisher named Fischer
Fished for fish from the edge of a fissure.

A fish with a grin
pulled the fisherman in!
Now they're hunting the fissure for Fischer.

Anonymous

Change the Word

1. Write two words that rhyme with **fish**.

2. Write a sentence using one of the words.

3. Write two words that rhyme with **grin**.

4. Write a sentence using one of the words.

Pizza Pie

Bite, chew, crunch and munch.
Pizza pie is great for lunch.
Top it off with fruity punch.
Oh my gosh! I ate a bunch!

Tim Rasinski

Pair 'Em Up

1. Cross out the word that does NOT belong.

crunch	bunch	shore
munch	church	punch
hunch	lunch	such

Word Meaning

2. Write the word from the box that matches the definition.

punch	bunch	munch

This word means **chew**. ______

This word means **a lot of something**. ______

This is a sweet drink. ______

Over the River and Through the Woods

Over the river and through the woods
To grandfather's house we go;
The horse knows the way to carry the sleigh,
Through the white and drifted snow.

Over the river and through the woods,
Oh how the wind does blow!
It stings the toes and bites the nose,
As over the ground we go.

Lydia Maria Child

Rhyming Words

1. Write a word from the poem that rhymes with each bold word.

The horse knows the **way**

To grandfather's house we **go**

It stings the **toes**

Think About It

2. What time of year does this poem take place?

3. Where are they going?

There Was an Old Woman

There was an old woman
    who lived in a shoe.
She had so many children,
    she didn't know what to do.
She gave them some broth,
    some fruit, and some bread,
Kissed them all sweetly
    and sent them to bed.

Adapted by Laura Portalupi

New Words

1. Add **-ing** to these words to make new words.
Say the new words.

do + ing

kiss + ing

send + ing

play + ing

Think About It

2. Write the foods the old woman gave to her children.

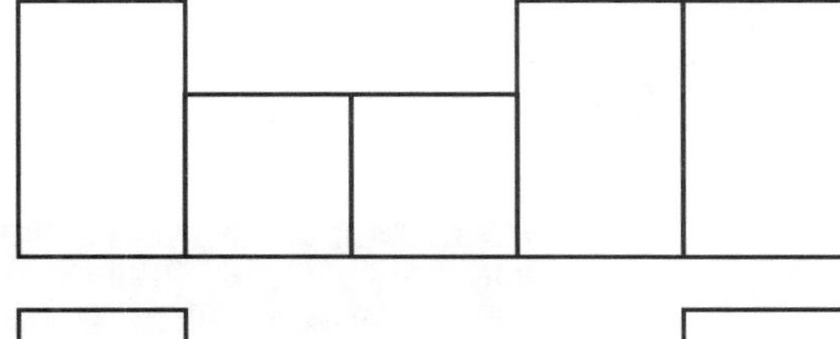

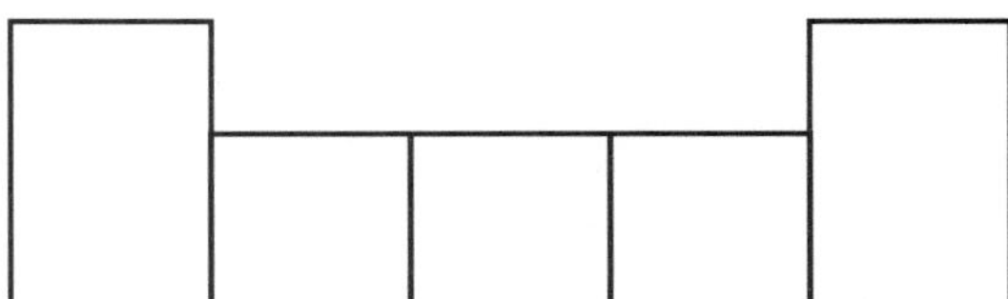

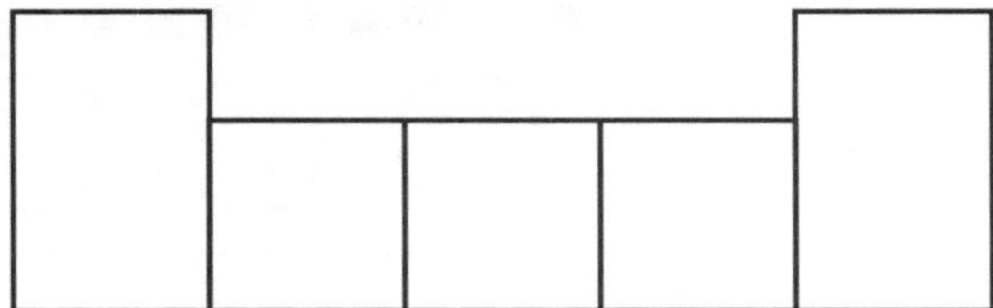

A Mouse

A mouse in her room woke Miss Dowd;
She was frightened and screamed very loud,
    Then a happy thought hit her—
    To scare off the critter,
She sat up in the bed and meowed.

Anonymous

Opposites

1. Draw a line to connect the opposites.

loud	sad
happy	fell asleep
woke	quiet
she	he

What Happens Next?

2. Draw a picture that shows what you think happens after Miss Dowd meowed.

The Little Turtle

There was a little turtle.
He lived in a box.
He swam in a puddle.
He climbed on the rocks.

He snapped at a mosquito.
He snapped at a flea.
He snapped at a minnow.
And he snapped at me.

He caught the mosquito.
He caught the flea.
He caught the minnow.
But he didn't catch me.

Vachel Lindsay

Rhyming Words

1. Circle three words that rhyme with **box**.

socks	fix	knocks	bowl	locks	mix

2. Circle the word that does NOT rhyme with **me**.

sea	my	free	tea	pea	bee

Change the Word

3. Write one word from the poem that answers each question.

Where did the little turtle swim? ______________

What did the little turtle climb on? ______________

Little Piece of Prickly Pear

Mama calls me her
    little piece of *prickly pear*
when I am sour,
    when I stamp my feet.

Mama calls me her little *tuna*,
    good enough to eat
when I am smiling,
    when I am sweet.

Tony Johnston

Draw a Picture

1. Draw a picture of yourself acting **sour**.

2. Draw a picture of yourself acting **sweet**.

The Pickety Fence

The pickety fence
The pickety fence
Give it a lick it's
The pickety fence

Give it a lick it's
A clickety fence
Give it a lick it's
A lickety fence
Give it a lick

Give it a lick
Give it a lick
With a rickety stick

Pickety
Pickety
Pickety
Pick

David McCord

Rhyming Words

1. Write two words from the poem that rhyme with **pick**.

2. Add the letters **-ety** to the two words above.

Word Endings

3. Write four words from the poem that end with **-ety**.

Rain

listen listen
listen to the rain
listen listen
listen to the rain
listen listen listen listen
listen to the rain

softer softer
listen to the rain
softer softer
listen to the rain
listen listen listen listen
listen to the rain

louder louder
listen to the rain
louder louder
listen to the rain
listen listen listen listen
listen to the rain

Sonja Dunn

Word Work

Shape Search

1. Write two words from the poem that begin with **l**.

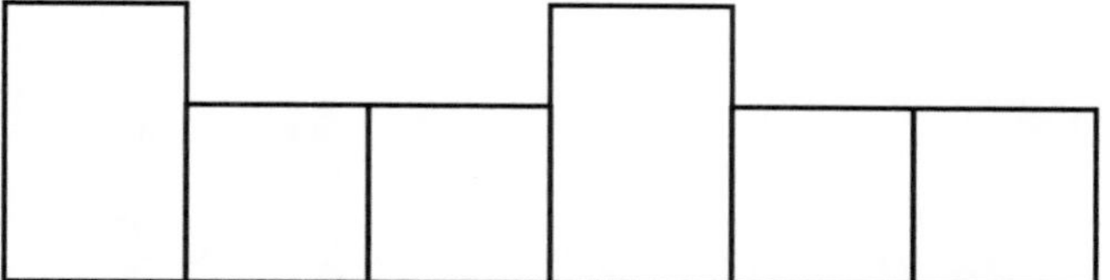

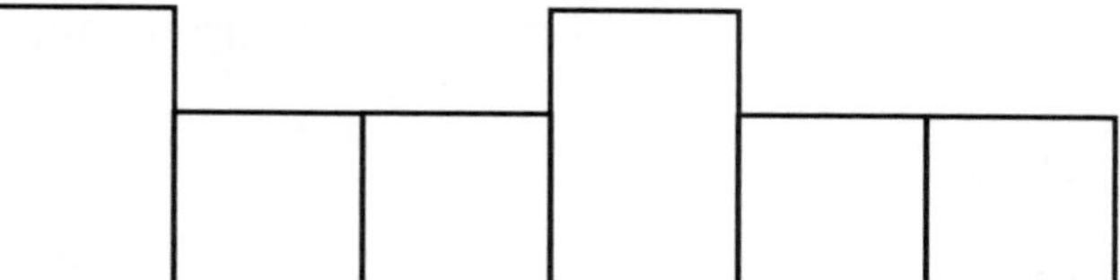

2. Write one word from the poem that begins with **s**.

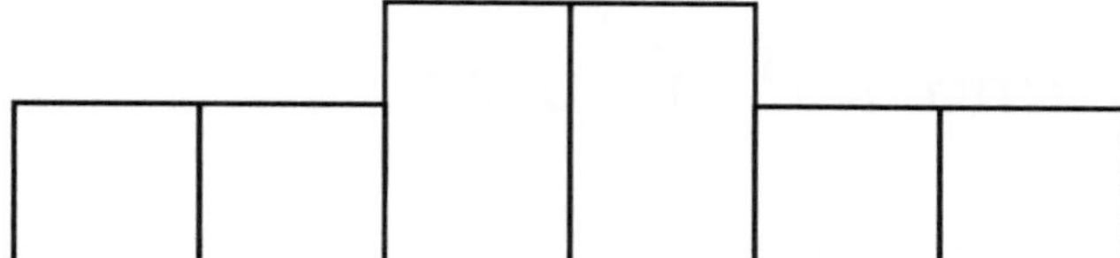

3. Write one word from the poem that begins with **r**.

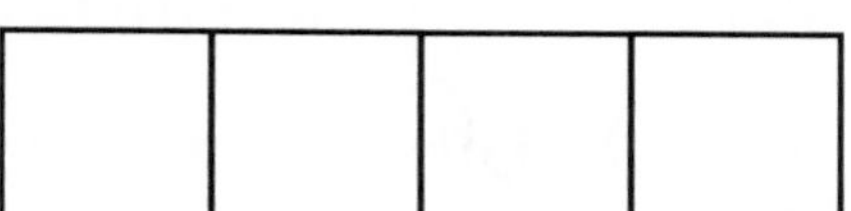

Softer and Louder

4. Circle the correct picture.

Which is softer?

Which is louder?

Which is louder?

Black, White, and Red Jokes

What's black and white and read all over?
    The newspaper.

What's black and white and red all over?
    A penguin with a sunburn.

What's black and white and red all over?
    A blushing panda.

Author unknown

Color Names

1. Write the names of the three colors used in the jokes.

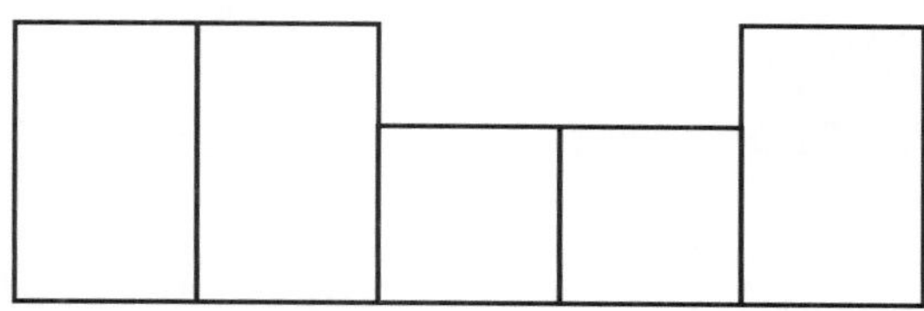

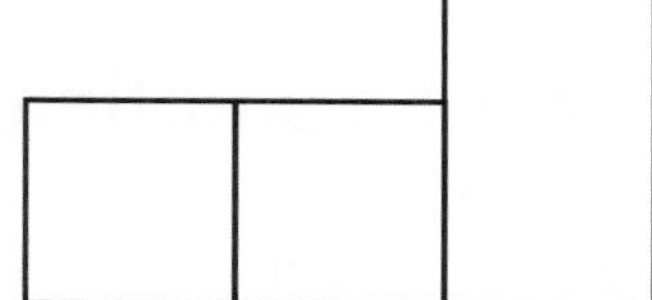

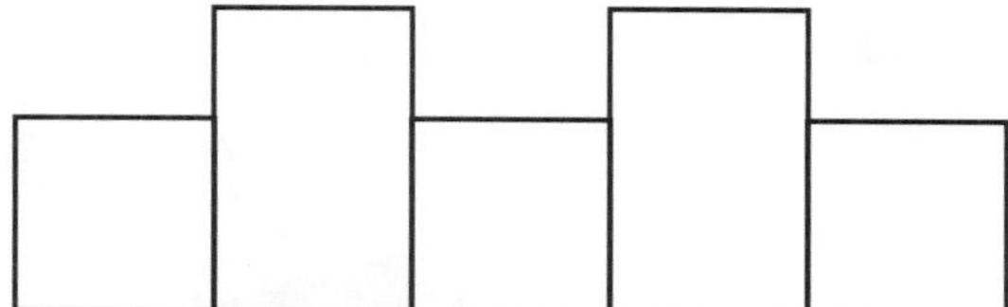

Picture Match

2. Write a word from the poem to match each picture.

Yo-yo

I have a yo-yo,
And I make it go go.
Sometimes real fast fast,
and sometimes real slow slow.

Sometimes it's high high
And sometimes it's low low.
Me and my yo-yo
put on a show show.

Karen McGuigan Brothers

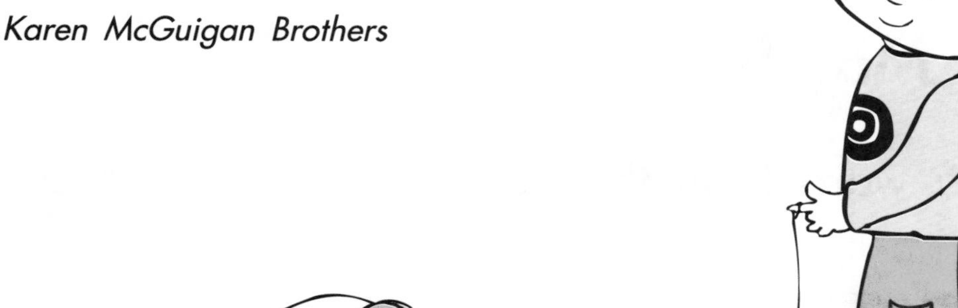

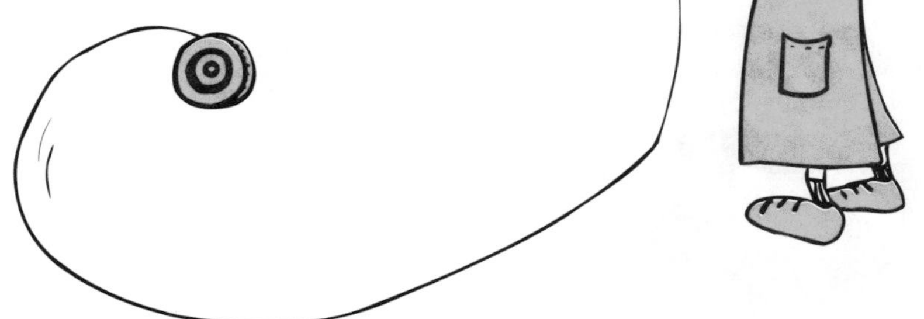

How did I read?

Movement Words

1. Write words from the poem that describe how a yo-yo moves.

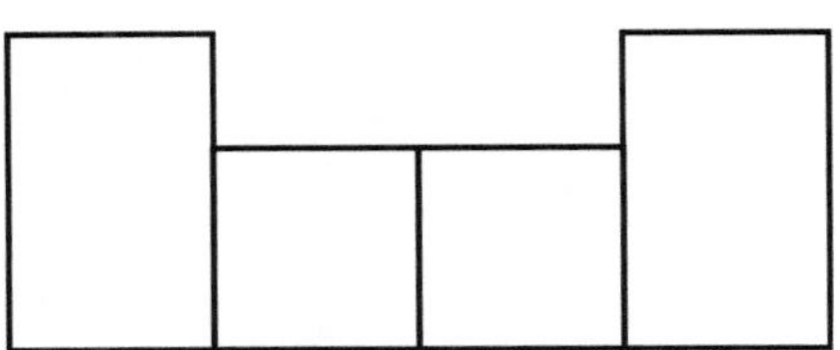

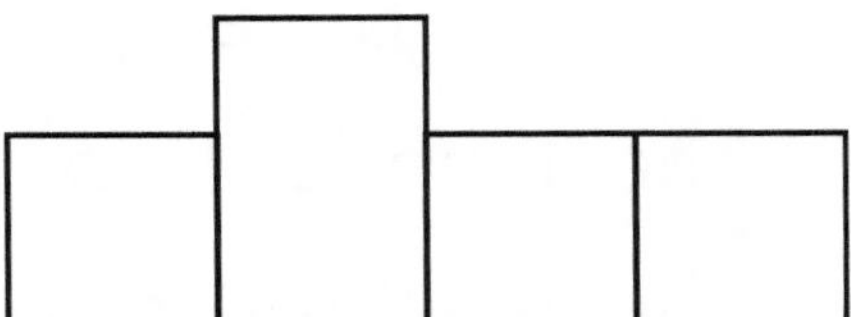

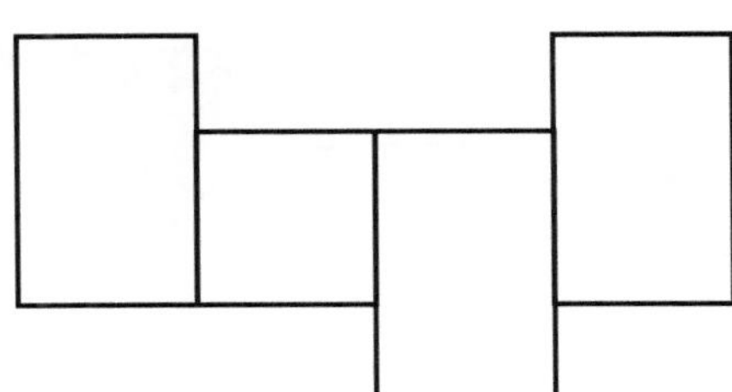

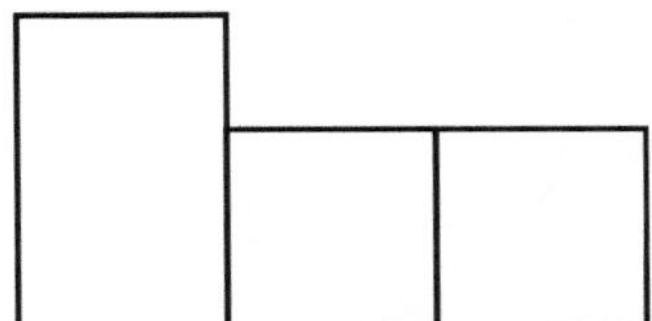

Compound Word

2. **Sometimes** is a compound word. Write the two small words that make up the compound.

Way Down South

Way down South
    where bananas grow,
A grasshopper stepped
    on an elephant's toe.
The elephant said,
    with tears in his eyes,
"Pick on somebody
    your own size."

Nursery rhyme

Name That

1. Write the names of the insect and animal in the poem.

g

e

Compound Words

2. Find the compound words in the poem. Write the two small words that make up the compound.

g h

s b

City Bus

Here we go
on the city bus
stopping at streets
yes, that's us
Going slow
Going fast
Hope this bus ride
will last and last

King Street
Queen Street
Front Street
Main
Mulberry
Cedar
Stop for a train

High Street
Low Street
Downtown mall
The city bus
will never stall

Up the parkway
Down the hill
We know the driver
His name is Bill

Over the bridge
to cross the river
I wish this ride
would last forever

Sonja Dunn

Shape Search

1. Write a word from the poem for each clue.

This street comes right after Main.

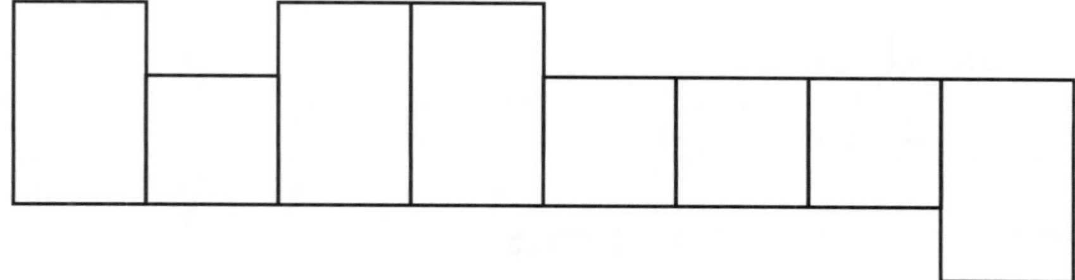

This street comes right before Low Street.

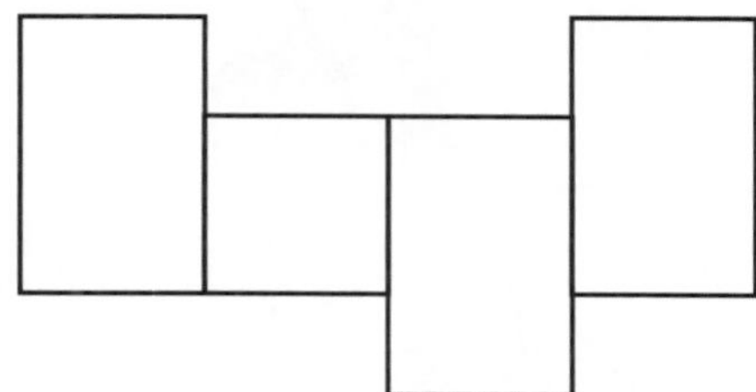

Compounds

2. Draw a line to make a compound word from the poem.

for	town
down	way
park	ever

There Was a Crooked Man

There was a crooked man
And he walked a crooked mile;
He found a crooked sixpence
Beside a crooked stile;
He bought a crooked cat
And it caught a crooked mouse
And they both lived together
In a wee crooked house.

Nursery rhyme

Rhyming Words

1. Write a word from the poem that rhymes with these words.

mile

caught

mouse

pound

Word Endings

2. Write four words that end with **-ook**.

Covers

Glass covers windows
    to keep the cold away

Clouds cover the sky
    to make a rainy day

Nighttime covers
    all the things that creep

Blankets cover me
    when I'm asleep

Nikki Giovanni

Word Endings

1. Write three words from the poem that end in **-eep**.

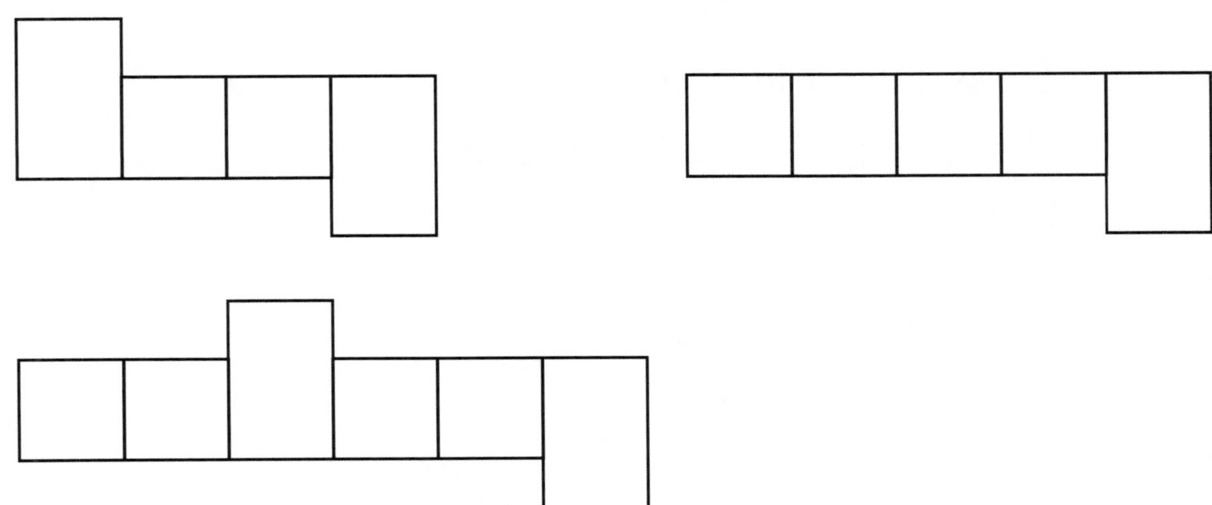

Word Endings

2. Write two words in the poem that end with **-ay**.

Write two more with the same ending.

A Cat Called Little Bell

Kitty, kitty, pretty thing—
Ting-a-ling a-ling a-ling.
Around your neck a little bell
Goes ting-a-ling a-ling a-ling.
That's why we call you Little Bell,
Kitty, kitty, pretty thing.

Traditional Japanese rhyme

Shape Search

1. Write two words from the poem that end in **-y**.

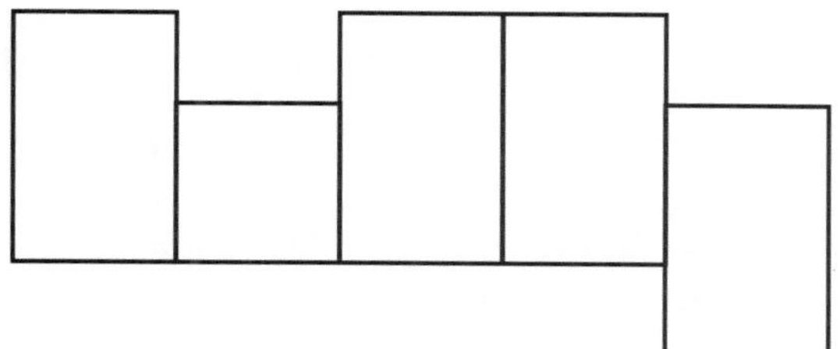

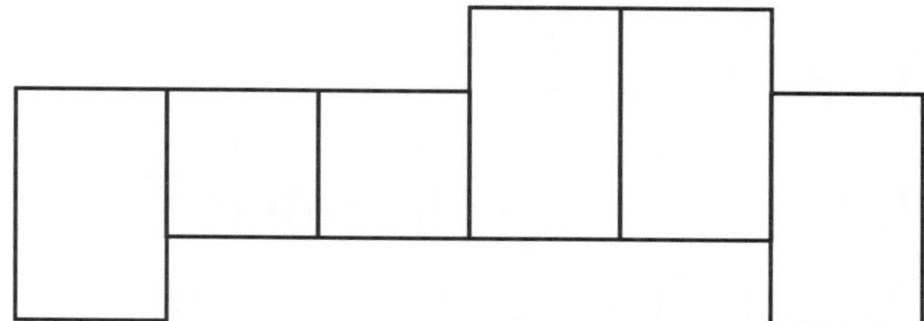

Word Match

2. Draw a line to match the words that belong together.

a name	Little Bell
a thing	little bell

Write a Sentence

3. Write a sentence about cats.

Over There

Over there, there is a park, where I go to play.
    Over where?
Over there.
    Over where?
Behind those trees.
    I can't see.
Behind those trees, there's swings and things.
    And jungle gyms and slides?

Yes, and grass and playing fields
    and seesaws you can ride.

Sarah Hutt

Word Search

1. Write a word from the poem to match the picture.

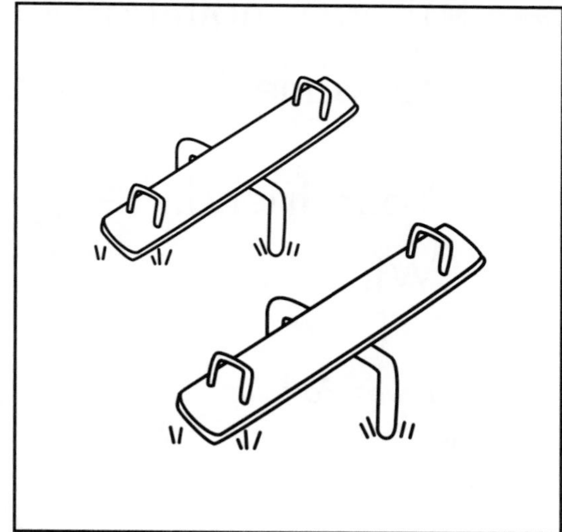

Word Patterns

2. Write a word from the poem that begins with **r** and has a **long i** sound.

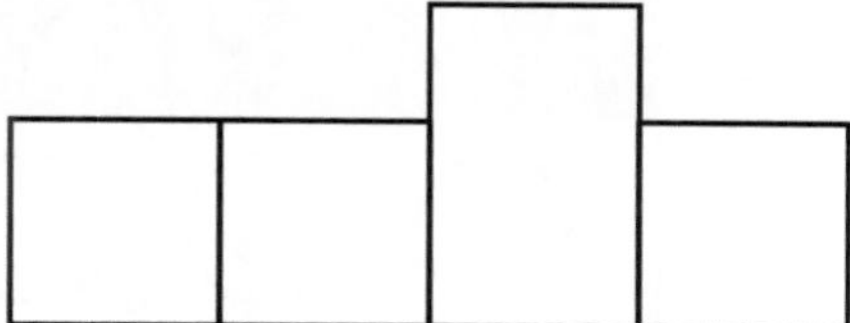

Dear Jill,

Thanks for the blueberry pie
you left on the windowsill.
There's nothing worse than cold, dry pie,
so while it was warm I ate my fill.

Your friend,
Will

Laura Portalupi

Word Search

1. Write a word from the letter that ends with the **long e** sound you hear in **me**.

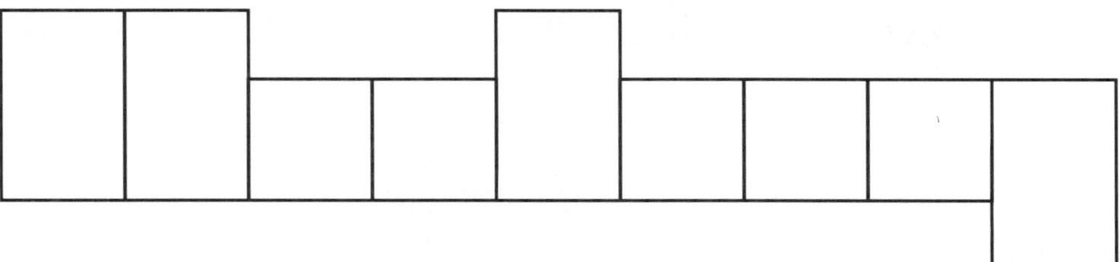

2. Write two words from the letter that end with the **long i** sound you hear in **pie**.

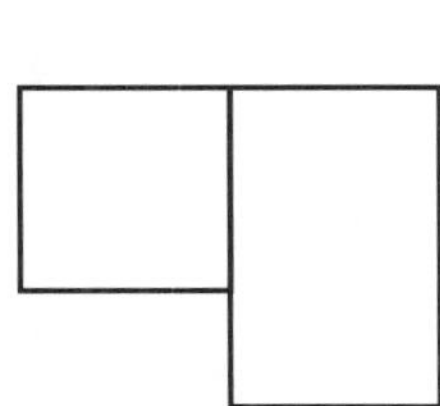

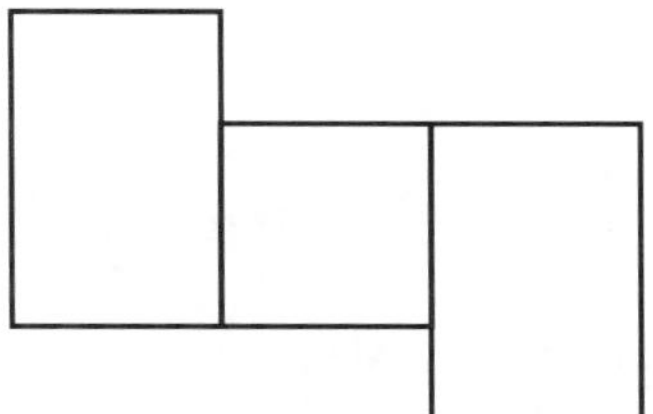

Making Words

3. Write three words from the letter that end with **-ill**.

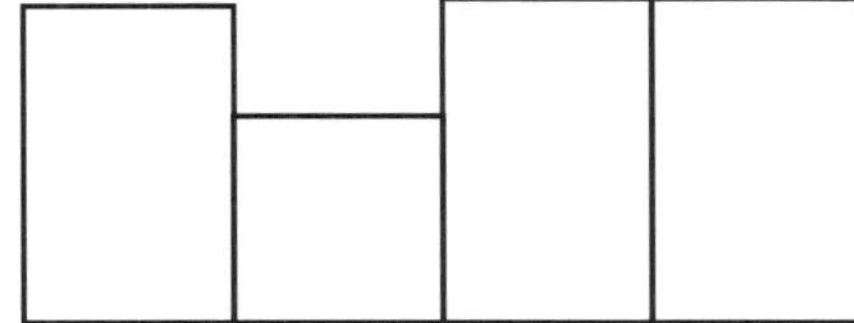

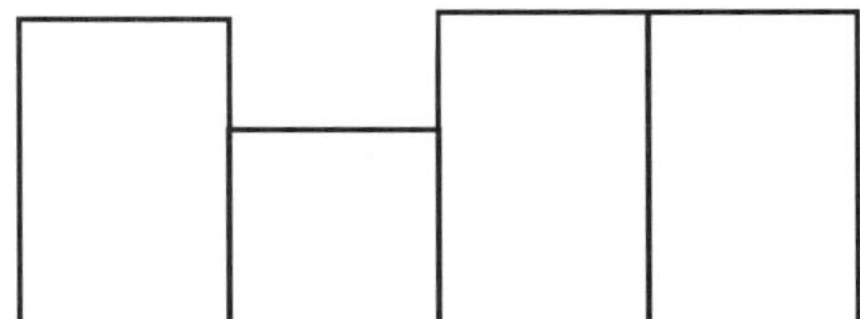

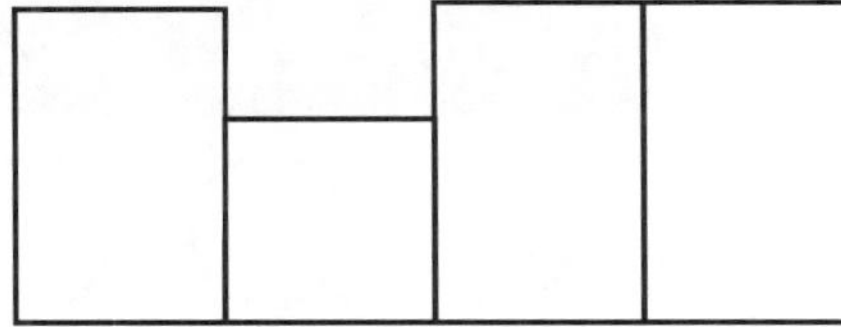

P-B-J

Peanut butter and jelly
(Grape Jelly!)
On white bread with the crusts cut off

P-B-J

Peanut butter and jelly
(Strawberry Jelly!)
On white bread with the crusts cut off

P-B-J
Peanut butter and jelly
(Raspberry Jelly!)
On white bread with the crusts cut off
(Don't forget the potato chips!)

Sarah Hutt

Word Work

Which Is Which?

1. Draw a line from the word or words from the story to the picture that matches.

bread

jelly

peanut butter

Shape Search

2. Write three words from the poem that have double letters two times in a row.

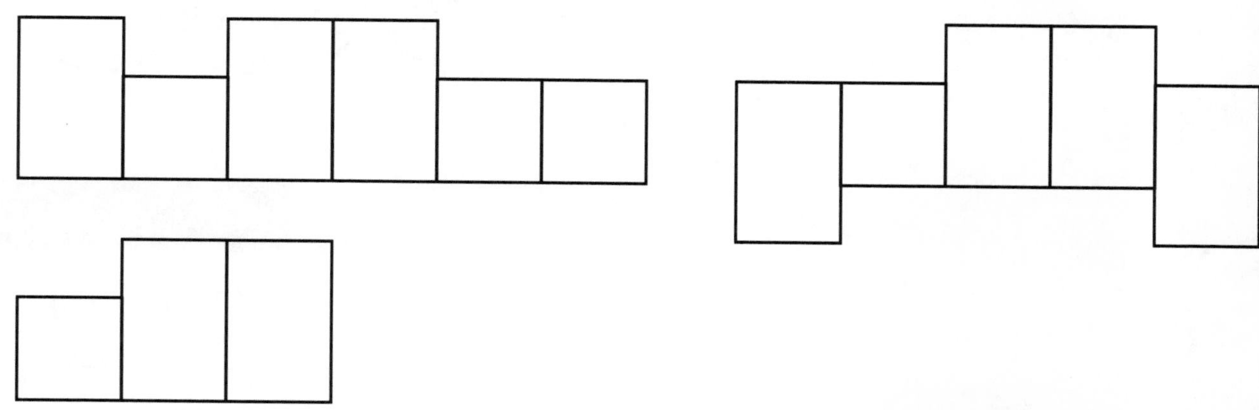

Goober Peas

Sitting by the roadside
    on a summer day,
Chatting with my good friends,
    passing time away,
Lying in the shadow
    underneath the trees,
Goodness, how delicious,
    eating goober peas!

Peas! Peas! Peas! Peas!
Eating goober peas!
Goodness, how delicious,
Eating goober peas!

Traditional American song

Beginning Sounds

1. Write three words from the poem that have the same beginning sound as **goat**.

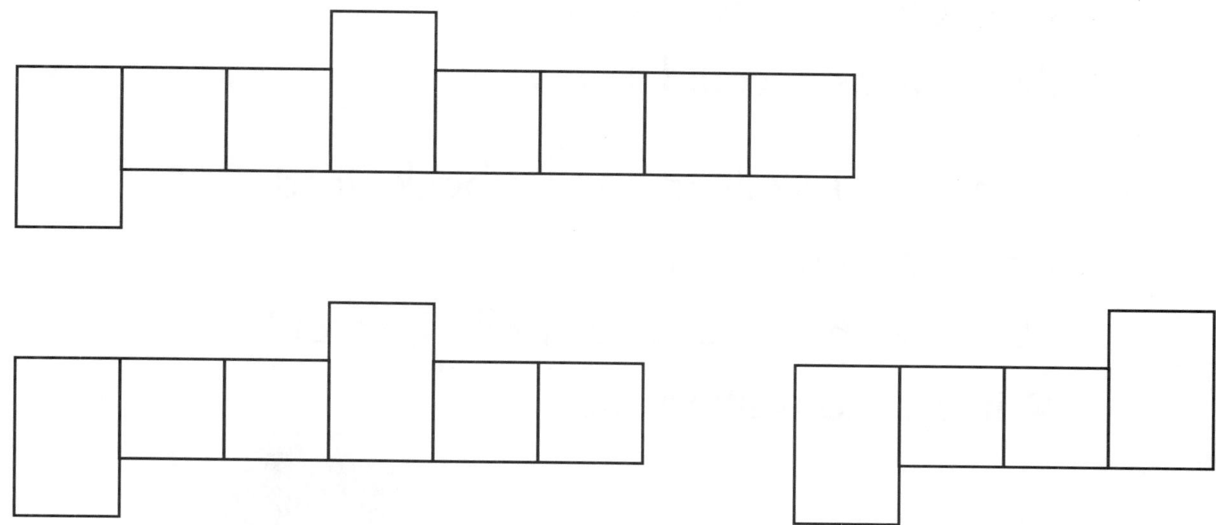

2. Write two words from the poem that have the same beginning sound as **dish**.

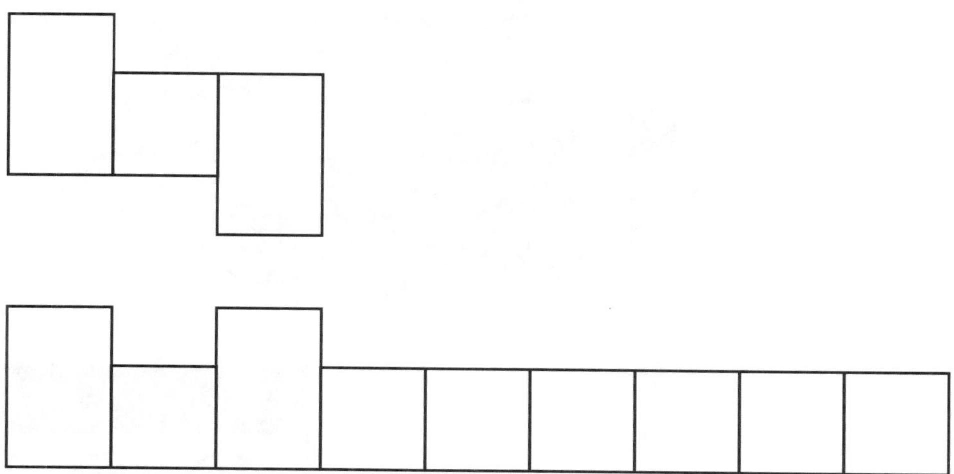

Tommy

I put a seed into the ground
And said, "I'll watch it grow."
I watered it and cared for it
As well as I could know.

One day I walked in my back yard,
And oh, what did I see!
My seed had popped itself right out,
Without consulting me.

Gwendolyn Brooks

Words With -eed

1. Use the letters in the box to make words that end with **-eed**.

n	s	w	f

______ ______ ______ ______

Words With -ow

2. Use the letters in the box to make words that end with **-ow**.

gr	t	kn	r

______ ______ ______ ______

Finish the Sentence

3. Fill in the blanks with words you made above.

My ______ will ______ into a flower.

My People

The night is beautiful,
So the faces of my people.

The stars are beautiful,
So the eyes of my people.

Beautiful, also, is the sun.
Beautiful, also, are the souls of my people.

Langston Hughes

Change the Word

1. Change the first letter in each word to make a word from the poem. Write it on the line.

fun ______________________

laces ______________________

light ______________________

Means the Same

2. Write a word from the poem that means the same as **pretty**.

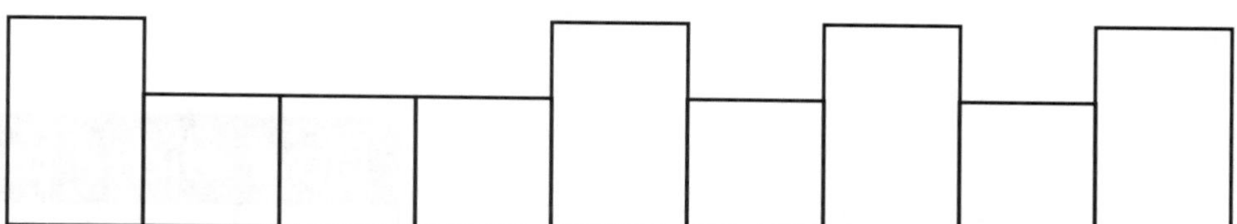

Whenever You Wink

Whenever you wink
there is a link
to the rest of your face
I suppose.

For when you wink
why do you think
it wrinkles up
your nose?

Karen McGuigan Brothers

Sounds the Same

1. Write the word from the poem that sounds the same, but is spelled differently.

two ____________ four ____________

their ____________ knows ____________

Word Meanings

2. Write words that end the same as **wink** and fit the definitions.

a color ____________

where you wash your hands ____________

what you do with milk ____________

Winter Is Coming

The wind will blow
  we will have snow.
The fish in the lake
  will swim way down low.

When the top turns to ice
  do they think it's nice?
When I'm skating there
  do they even know?

Karen McGuigan Brothers

Match the Picture

1. Circle the word that matches the picture.

down blow

fish flip

snow slow

low ice

Rhyming Words

2. Draw a line to connect the rhyming words.

nice	low
know	late
lake	mice
skate	snake

Every Six Months

I went to the dentist
to get checked out.

The dentist said, "Kelly
open your mouth.

You've brushed and flossed
after eating cheese.

That's why you have
NO CAVITIES."

Sonja Dunn

How did I read?

Rhyming Words

1. Write a word from the poem that rhymes with **please**.

2. Circle the word that does not rhyme with the others.

crossed tossed flossed toast

Change the Word

3. Change the first letter in each word to make a word from the poem. Write it on the line.

sent

south

crushed

Leaky Boots

Squish-squash, split-splat
    Squoosh, squoosh, squash

I sprang a leak in puddles deep,
    in my right galosh.

Now I have to walk back home,
    my shoes all filled with muck.

On rainy days, when I'm all wet,
    I wish I were a duck!

Sarah Hutt

How did I read?

☺ ☺ 😐

Change the Word

1. Change the vowel in each word to make a word from the poem. Write it on the line.

squish ______________________

split ______________________

spring ______________________

Rhyming Words

2. Circle the words in each box that rhyme.

squish	squash	dish

squash	wash	sprang

The Tutor

A tutor who tooted the flute
    Tried to tutor two tooters to toot.
Said the two to the tutor,
    "Is it harder to toot or
To tutor two tooters to toot?"

Author unknown

Odd Word Out

1. Circle the two words that have the same **oo** sound.

toot cook moon

Sounds the Same

2. Write a word from the poem that sounds the same as this word, but is spelled differently.

tooter

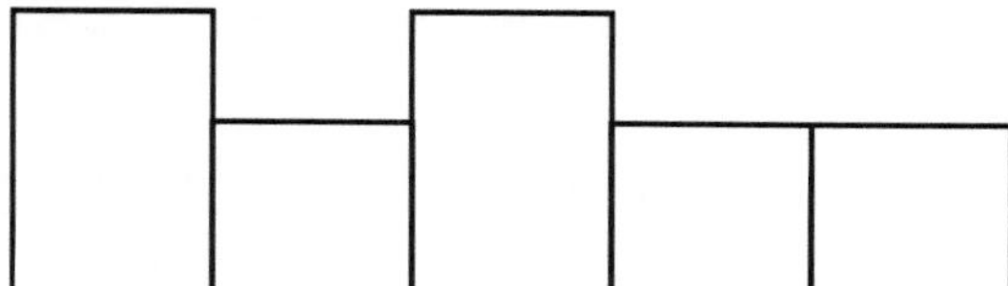

Means the Same

3. Write a word from the poem that means the same as this word.

teacher

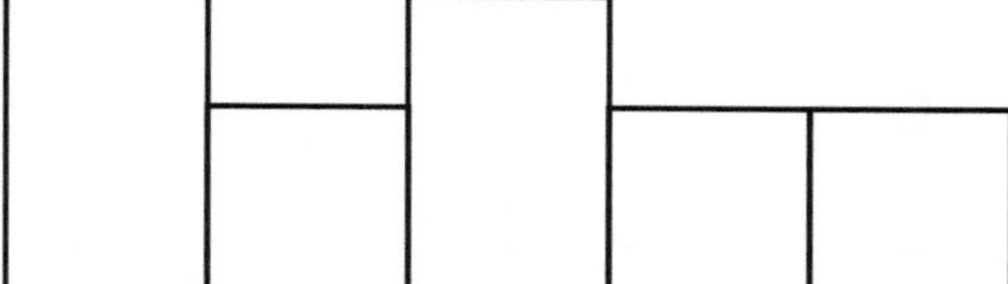

It All Adds Up

Once there was a lonely son,
Sad 'cause he was only one.

Then along came Cindy Lou,
Now there were a happy two!

Next they met Joanne Marie.
That made them a cheerful three!

Then along came Salvador,
Now they were a friendly four!

Soon they saw Roberto Clive.
That made them a classy five!

Next they went to play at Nick's,
Where they became a joyful six!

Then along came Kenneth Kevin.
That made them a cozy seven!

Soon they met Melissa Kate,
Now they were an eager eight!

Along the road came Caroline.
That made them a nifty nine!

Finally they all met Gwen,
Ending up a perfect ten!

Author unknown

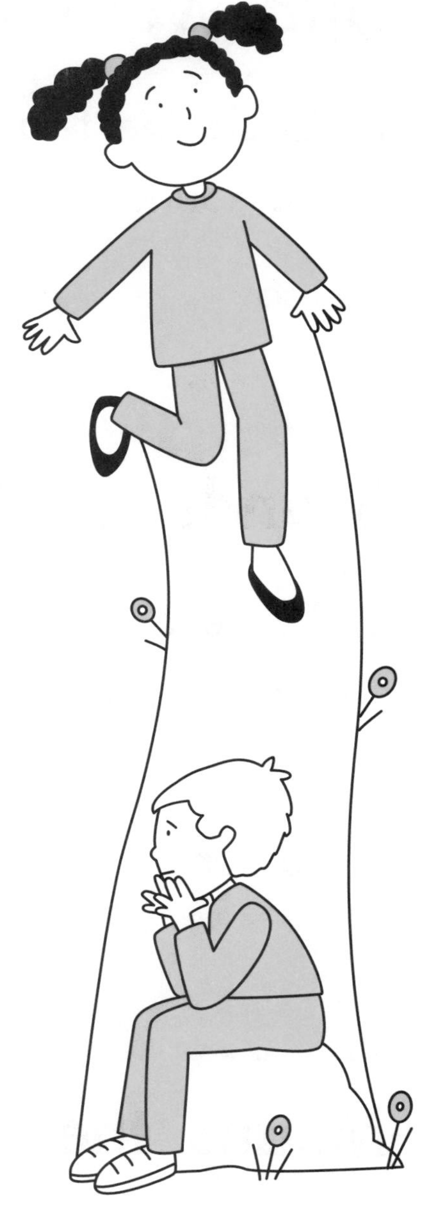

Change the Word

1. Change the beginning letter in each word to make a word from the poem.

toad

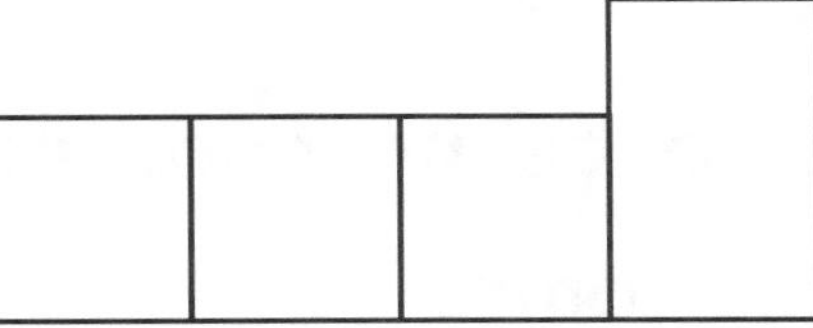

fifty

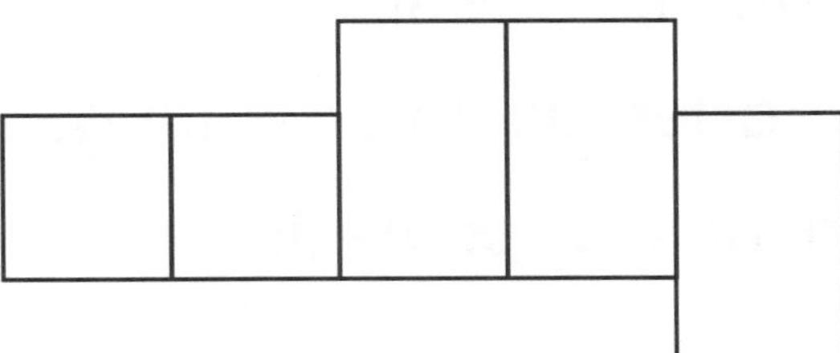

Match the Names

2. Draw a line from each number word to the name that matches.

two	Nick's
four	Cindy Lou
six	Melissa Kate
eight	Gwen
ten	Salvador

Rainy Day

Trickle, splat, bang!
Here comes the thunder and pouring rain
Harder, faster, wetter it falls
There seems to be no end...no end at all
Wait! Here it comes!
The storm has cleared,
At last, after all this waiting,
The sun has appeared!

Lisa Rasback

Rhyming Words

1. Circle three words that rhyme with **all**.

talk	call	sale	small	hall	nail

2. Circle two words that rhyme with **cleared**.

appeared	pear	wear	feared

Word Meanings

3. Write words that end with **-end** and fit the definitions.

a turn in the road ______________________

to mail a letter or package ______________________

to fix something ______________________

Kookaburra

Kookaburra sits in the old gum tree.
Merry, merry king of the bush is he.
Laugh, Kookaburra,
Laugh, Kookaburra,
Glad your life must be.

Kookaburra sits in the old gum tree,
Eating all the gumdrops he can see.
Stop, Kookaburra,
Stop, Kookaburra,
Leave some there for me.

Marion Sinclair

How did I read?

Vowel Sounds

1. Circle the words from the poem with short vowel sounds.

sits	old	gum	tree

bush	is	he	glad

Opposites

2. Draw a line to match each word from the poem to its opposite.

sits	go
glad	sad
stop	new
old	stands

Four Seasons

Spring is showery, flowery, bowery.
Summer is hoppy, croppy, poppy.
Autumn is wheezy, sneezy, freezy.
Winter is slippy, drippy, nippy.

Showery hoppy wheezy slippy
Flowery croppy sneezy drippy
Bowery poppy freezy nippy
I love how the seasons change.

Anonymous

Words Inside Words

1. Write the small word that you find in each word below.

hoppy ______ croppy ______

slippy ______ poppy ______

drippy ______ showery ______

nippy ______ flowery ______

freezy ______ winter ______

Castle-Building

I built a big castle.
It looked so very grand.
I built it on the beach.
I made it out of sand.

But suddenly a wave came in
and washed it all away.
I'll build an even bigger one,
perhaps another day.

Karen McGuigan Brothers

How did I read?

☺ ☺ 😐

Word Sort

1. Write words from the poem to complete the chart. Write one or two of your own.

Short a sound	**Long a** sound

Sorry, Sorry Mrs. Lorry

Sorry, sorry Mrs. Lorry
couldn't keep from being sorry.

Broke a plate,
"So sorry, Kate!"
Tripped the cat,
"So sorry, Nat!"
Missed the bus,
"So sorry, Gus!"
"Guess I'm late.
I broke Kate's plate
And tripped Nat's Cat
Imagine that!"
Sorry, sorry Mrs. Lorry.

Nanette Mellage

Word Sort

1. Write words from the poem to complete the chart.

Names of people	Names of things

Rhyming Words

2. For each word, write another word from the poem that rhymes with it. Then write one of your own.

Nat

plate

Two Tongue Twisters

Which way will the wide walrus waddle
when we give him a watermelon?
We'll watch him wiggle, waddle,
wade into the water then fade away.

Twice I thought I saw two mice,
sitting in a chair with cheese.
I saw them gobble gulps of food,
so fast it made them sneeze.

Sarah Hutt

How did I read?

Draw a Picture

1. Draw what happens in one of the tongue twisters.

Sing a Song of Sixpence

Sing a song of sixpence,
    a pocket full of rye,
Four and twenty blackbirds
    baked in a pie,
When the pie was open
    the birds began to sing,
Wasn't that a dainty dish
    to set before a king?

The King was in his counting-house,
    counting out his money,
The Queen was in the parlor,
    eating bread and honey,
The maid was in the garden,
    hanging out the clothes,
Along came a blackbird and
    pecked at her nose.

Nursery rhyme

Living or Not?

1. Use the words in the box to complete the chart.

bird	pie	dish	king
queen	money	maid	clothes

Living things	Non-living things

Oh! How I Hate to Get Up in the Morning

Oh! how I hate to get up in the morning,
Oh! how I'd love to remain in bed;

For the hardest blow of all
is to hear the bugler call:

You've got to get up,
You've got to get up,
You've got to get up this morning!

Irving Berlin

How did I read?

Opposites

1. Write a word that means the opposite of each word.

hate

soft

Wake-Up Call

2. How do you get up in the morning? Draw a picture and write about it.

Beetle Thoughts

What do beetles think about
    in places where they crawl?
Are their thoughts in April
    like the thoughts they have in fall?

No one knows what beetles think,
    but if they think at all
I think the thoughts that beetles think
    must be very small.

Aileen Fisher

Shape Search

1. Write three words from the poem that begin with **th**.

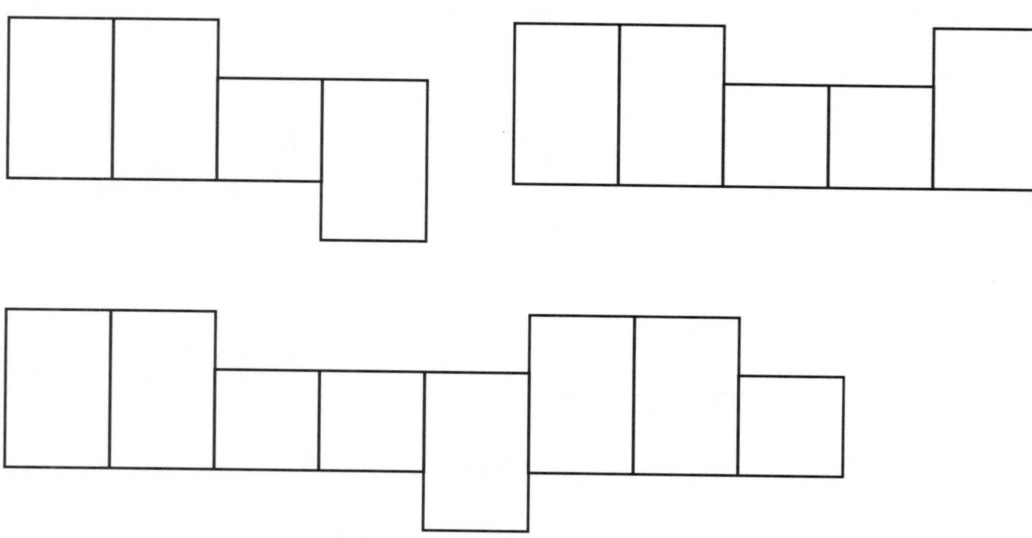

Think About It

2. If a beetle could think, what would it think about? Write your ideas here.

Pot Roast

Pot roast,
French toast,
Vacations on the sea coast,
School bells, sea shells—
These are the things I like the most!

Lima beans,
Green beans,
Much-too-tight blue jeans,
Being told to clean my plate—
These are the things I really hate!

Karen McGuigan Brothers

Word Work

Likes

1. Circle three things from the poem that the speaker likes.

pot roast	sea shells	earrings	school bells

2. Write two things you like.

Dislikes

3. Circle three things from the poem that the speaker does NOT like.

green beans	broccoli	tight jeans	lima beans

4. Write two things you do NOT like.

All Aboard

All Aboard!
Let's sail across the sea.

Look! A big wave!
Let's sail over it.

Hold on tight.
SLIPPY, SLAPPY, SLOP!

Look! A storm!
Let's sail through it.

Cover up.
PLIPPY, PLAPPY, PLOP!

Look! A rainbow!
Let's sail under it.

Reach up high.
TIPPY, TAPPY, TOP!

Fay Robinson

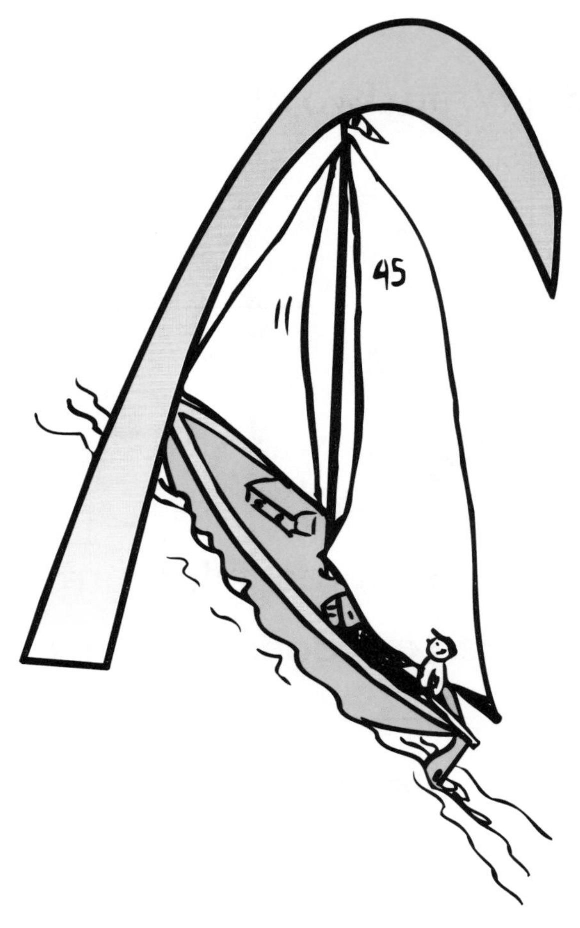

Opposites

1. Write a word from the poem that means the opposite of each word below.

under ____________ loose ____________

down ____________ low ____________

Make New Words

2. Write a word from the poem to make a compound word.

a kind of boat ____________boat

something you find in the sand ____________shell

rooms on the second floor ____________stairs

freeway; main road ____________way

An Irish Well Wish

May your thoughts be
as glad as the shamrocks,
May your heart be
as light as a song,
May each day bring you
bright, happy hours,
That stay with you all the year long.

Author unknown

How did I read?

Syllable Count

1. Write two words from the wish that have two syllables.

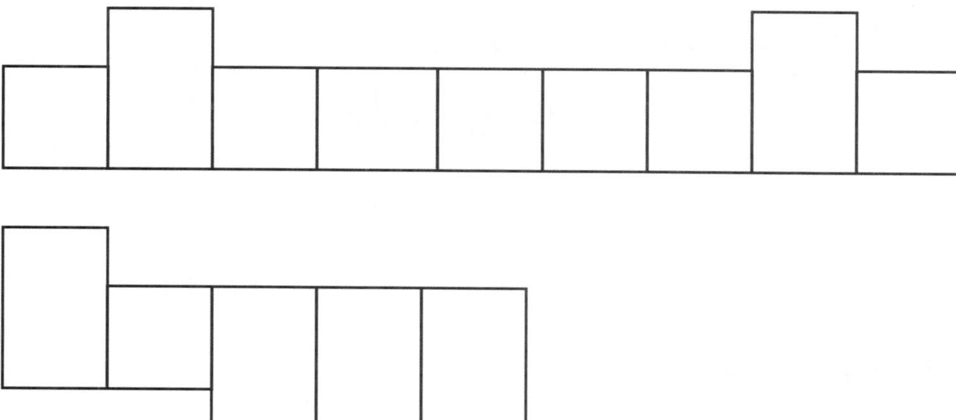

Write a Wish

2. Write your own well wish.

A Limerick

Said the snail to the tortoise: "You may
Find it hard to believe what I say;
    You will think it absurd,
    But I give you my word,
They fined me for speeding today."

"Well, well!" said the tortoise. "Dear me!"
How defective your motor must be!
    Though I speed every day,
    Not a fine do I pay:
The police cannot catch me, you see."

Oliver Herford

Long Sounds

1. Write words from the box to complete the chart.

me	may	say	be	pay	see

Long a words	**Long e** words

Word Meanings

2. Look at the first word in each row below. Circle the word next to it that is closest in meaning.

absurd	about	silly
defective	bad	deep

Sippity Sup

Sippity sup, sippity sup,
Bread and milk from a china cup.
Bread and milk from a bright silver spoon
Made of a piece of the bright silver moon.
Sippity sup, sippity sup,
Sippity, sippity sup.

Nursery rhyme

How did I read?

☺ ☺ 😐

Rhyming Words

1. Use the words from the box that rhyme with **spoon** and **moon** to answer the riddles. Write the answers on the lines.

noon	June	balloon	dune	soon

I'm coming back ________________.

I'm a time of day. ________________

I'm a summer month. ________________

Grab the string, or I'll float away! ________________

You'll get sandy if you climb on me. ________________

What Do You See in the Heavens Bright?

What do you see in the heavens bright?
    I see the moon and the stars at night.
What do you see in the earth, pray tell?
    I see in the earth a deep, deep well.
What do you see in the well, my dear?
    I see a frog and his voice I hear.
What is he saying there on the rock?
    Get up, get up, ke'rh kua, ke'rh kua.

Chinese rhyme

How did I read?

Word Work

What Do You See?

1. Write two things from the poem that you see in the sky at night.

Sounds Like

2. The frog in the poem makes the sound **ke'rh kua**. Write the names of three animals. Then write the sound each animal makes.

Animal	Sound

Mr. Nobody

I know a funny little man,
As quiet as a mouse,
Who does the mischief that is done
In everybody's house!

There's no one ever sees his face
And yet we all agree
That every plate we break was cracked
By Mr. Nobody.

The finger marks upon the door
By none of us are made;
We never leave the blinds unclosed;
To let the curtains fade.

The ink we never spill; the boots
That lying round you see
Are not our boots; they all belong
To Mr. Nobody.

Author unknown

Rhyming Words

1. Write two words from the poem that rhyme with each word.

free

grade

Who Is Mr. Nobody?

2. Write who you think Mr. Nobody is. Then read your idea to a partner. Listen to your partner's idea. Do the two of you agree?

Andre

I had a dream last night. I dreamed
I had to pick a Mother out.
I had to choose a Father too.
At first, I wondered what to do,
There were so many there, it seemed,
Short and tall and thin and stout.

But just before I sprang awake,
I knew what parents I would take.

And this surprised and made me glad:
They were the ones I always had!

Gwendolyn Brooks

Opposites

1. Write a word from the poem for each clue.

Clue: This word means the opposite of **thin**.

Clue: This word means the opposite of **short**.

Making Words

2. Follow the directions. Start by using a word from the poem.

Write a word that means **not tall**.

Change a letter in the word above to make a word that means **to yell**.

Change a letter in the word above to make a word that means **not thin**.

Table Manners

The Goops they lick their fingers,
　　And the Goops they lick their knives,
They spill their broth on the tablecloth;
　　Oh, they lead disgusting lives!

The Goops they talk while eating,
　　And loud and fast they chew;
And that is why I'm glad that I
　　Am not a Goop—are you?

Gelett Burgess

How did I read?

☺ ☺ 😐

Add a Word

1. Read the words. Add two words from the poem that have the same vowel sound.

map last

him since

Tell the Truth!

2. The Goops lick their fingers and talk when they eat. Write what you do when you eat.

I Had a Little Puppy

I had a little puppy, his name was Tiny Tim,
I put him in the bathtub, to see if he could swim,
He drank all the water, he ate a bar of soap,
The next thing you know he had
    a bubble in his throat.

In came the doctor, in came the nurse,
In came the lady with the alligator purse,
Out went the doctor, out went the nurse,
Out went the lady with the alligator purse.

I kissed the doctor, I kissed the nurse,
And then I paid the lady
    with the alligator purse.

Jump rope rhyme

How did I read?

☺ ☺ 😐

Change the Word

1. Write two words from the poem that rhyme with each word.

worse

him

Write About It

2. Write a few sentences about the story.

Fruit Salad

Yellow and green, yellow and green.
Yummy, yummy, yellow and green.

Pick a yellow, pick a green.
Apples, apples, yellow and green.

Green and red, green and red.
Yummy, yummy, green and red.

Pick a green, pick a red.
Grapes, grapes, green and red.

Mix it up, mix it up.
Yummy, yummy, mix it up.

Some for me, some for you.
Fruit salad, fruit salad, for me and you.

Anastasia Suen

Word Work

Label the Picture

1. Write a word from the poem that names each picture.

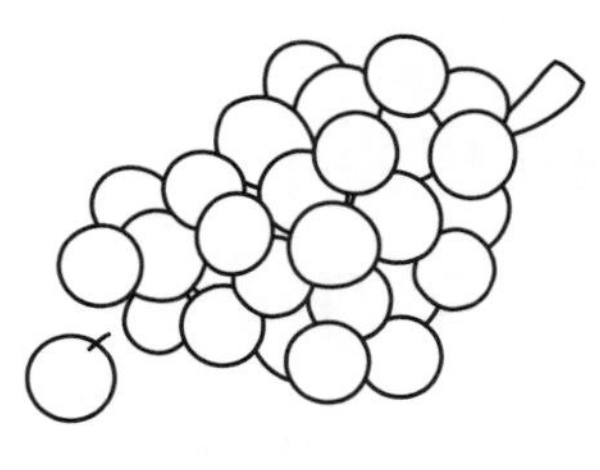

Color Names

2. Write the names of the three colors used in the poem.

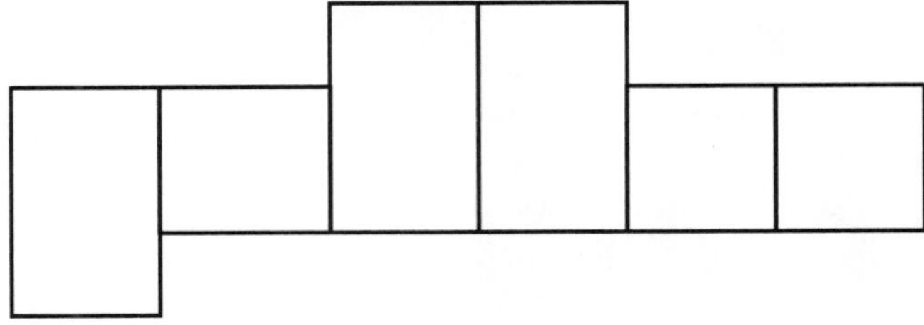

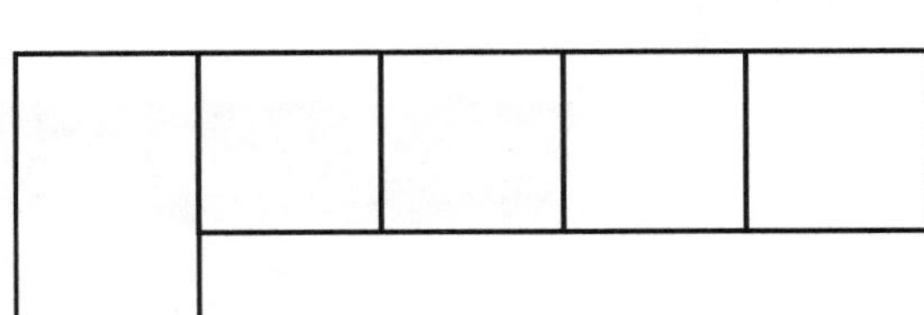

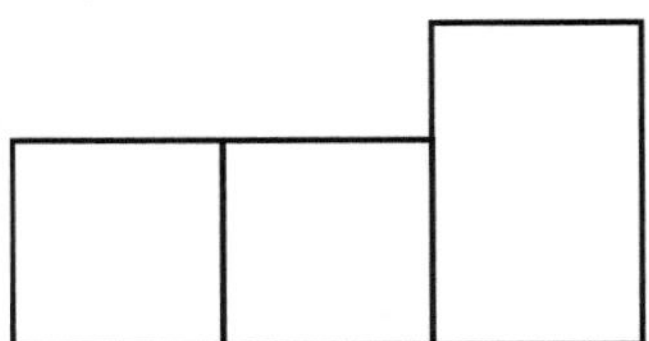

Five Little Bats

Five little bats hanging upside down,
The first one didn't make a sound.
The second one said, "I'll fly far tonight."
The third one said, "I don't like sunlight."
The fourth one said, "I want some bugs."
The fifth one said, "Let me give you a hug."
Five little bats hanging upside down.
Shhh! It's daytime, don't make a sound.

Author unknown

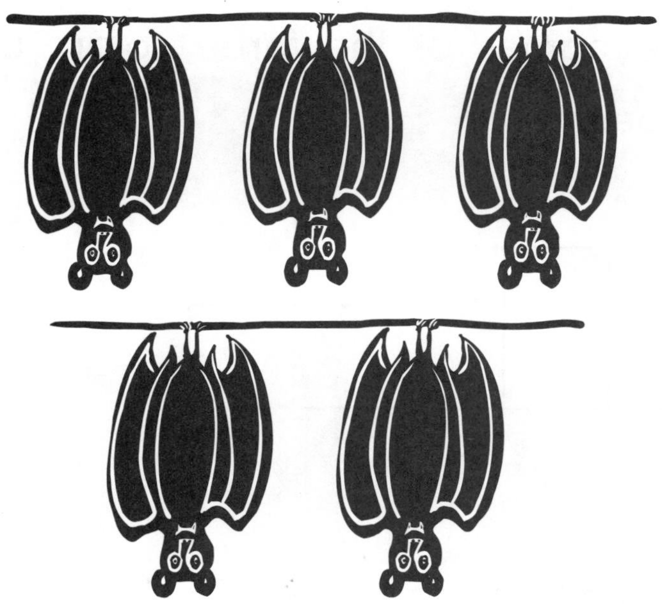

Order Words

1. Follow the directions using the order words.

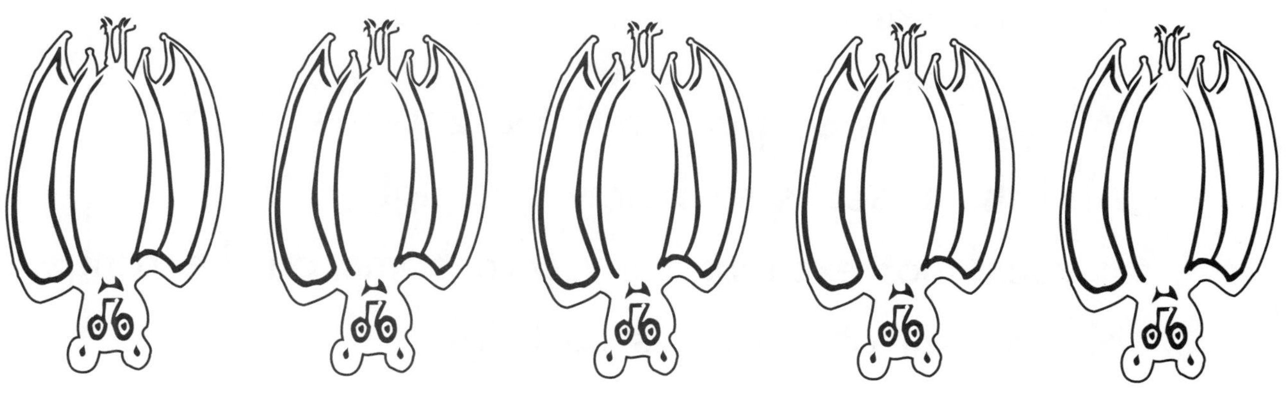

Color the second bat black.

Circle the first bat.

Color the fifth bat brown.

Cross out the third bat.

Draw a bug on the fourth bat.

Home on the Range

Oh, give me a home where the buffalo roam,
Where the deer and the antelope play,
Where seldom is heard a discouraging word,
And the skies are not cloudy all day.

Where air is so pure and the zephyrs so free
And the breezes so balmy and light,
I would not exchange my own home on the range,
Not for all of the cities so bright.

Home, home on the range,
Where the deer and the antelope play,
Where seldom is heard a discouraging word,
And the skies are not cloudy all day.

Dr. Brewster M. Higley

Word Work

Pair 'Em Up

1. Circle two words in each row that rhyme.

home	same	roam
cared	heard	word

Word Meaning

2. Write a word from the box that matches each definition.

seldom	range	exchange	roam

not very often ____________________

to trade ____________________

to wander around ____________________

open land where cattle live ____________________

Goodbye

Goodbye
Goodbye
Goodbye
Adios
So long
Farewell
Ciao
Ta ta
and au revoir
my friend
this is
the

E
N
D

Sonja Dunn

Matching Words

1. Write words from the poem that sound the same as these, but are spelled differently.

sew

good buy

fair well

Rhyming Words

2. Circle the word that does not rhyme.

end	spend	band	friend

my	pie	free	sky